THE BIBLE TIME

Explore the Bible

written by Mikal Keefer
illustrated by Carl Moore

STANDARD PUBLISHING
Cincinnati, Ohio

It all started one day when Shawn bought a new doghouse for Gizmo at a local garage sale.
Sure, it was a little funny looking, but it was a great bargain!
Everything seemed normal for a while, until we noticed that Gizmo was burying dinosaur bones in the backyard.
DOESN'T LOOK LIKE ANY DOGHOUSE *I'VE* EVER SEEN.
GiZMo's HoUSe
THE DOG DOESN'T LOOK TOO NORMAL, EITHER.

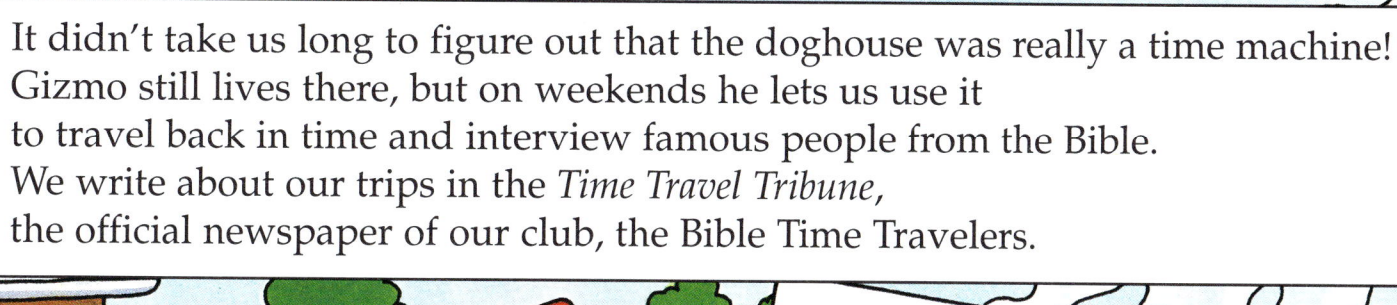

It didn't take us long to figure out that the doghouse was really a time machine! Gizmo still lives there, but on weekends he lets us use it to travel back in time and interview famous people from the Bible. We write about our trips in the *Time Travel Tribune*, the official newspaper of our club, the Bible Time Travelers.

TIME TRAVEL TRIBUNE

The Bible Time Travelers Visit Noah's Famous Ark

WEATHER FORECAST: Looks like 40 days and nights of rain!

For our next issue of the *Time Travel Tribune*, we decided to do an in-depth story about the Bible. We wanted to interview some of the people who helped to write it. And the only way to do that was to take another trip into the past!

Before take-off, everyone had a job to do. Chen studied the maps, Shawn logged onto the computer, Marcie adjusted the viewscreen, and Andy set our destination. When everyone was ready, Gizmo pushed the launch button and we blasted back in time to our first stop—Mount Sinai.

DESTINATION: 14000.0 BC

After Gizmo landed the time machine, we went out looking for Moses. When we finally caught up with him, he was coming down the mountain with two stone tablets in his arms.
ARE YOU MOSES?
YES.
ARE THOSE THE 10 COMMANDMENTS?
HOW DID **YOU** KNOW?
UMMM... LUCKY GUESS?

Moses told us all about the Ten Commandments that God gave him on top of the mountain. The new laws told everyone how to please God. But Moses couldn't stay and talk with us very long. He wanted to show the new laws to all his friends.

Moses wrote the first five books of the Bible. These books tell us about the creation of the world, Noah and the flood, the Hebrews' escape from Egypt, and lots of other cool stuff.

TIME TRAVEL TRIBUNE

Moses Brings God's New Laws Down Mountain on Stone Tablets

The Bible Time Travelers were on the scene when Moses brought the now-famous Ten Commandments down from a mountaintop.

"God gave me these laws to bring to his people," said Moses in an exclusive interview. "They are ten very special Commandments that will help us live better lives and please God."

Even though Moses was excited about the new laws, he was glad that they were written on just two tablets.

"God carved the laws on stones," said Moses. "If there were any more, I don't think I could have carried them."

Time Travelers Visit Past

Meeting Moses was great, but we were just getting started! So we blasted off again in search of more interviews.

Books That Moses Wrote

Genesis
Exodus
Leviticus
Numbers
Deuteronomy

At our next stop, we met a shepherd boy who was busy practicing with his sling. He looked like he was a pretty good shot, so we decided to stick around and watch.

THINK YOU COULD HIT A BEAR WITH YOUR SLINGSHOT?

SURE.

A LION?

YEP.

GOLIATH?

WHAT'S A GOLIATH?

YOU'LL SEE...

The young shepherd's name was David. Besides being good with a sling, David was also a very talented musician. Whenever he wasn't busy with his sheep, he was writing songs of praise to God. His best songs can be found in the book of Psalms.

Music Review
by Andy

Hello, music lovers. Today I am reviewing the best collection of songs ever written: the book of Psalms.

There are 150 songs in this book, and most of them were written by David. His songs are full of praise and love for God. Millions of people have enjoyed these songs over the years, which definitely puts them on the all-time best-seller list!

I really liked the book of Psalms, and I think you will, too. Check it out!

Book of Psalms ★★★★★

We visited King Solomon in his royal palace. During his time, he was the richest man in the whole world. He was also the wisest.

Advice Column
by Marcie

Dear Marcie,
Do I *really* have to listen to my parents?
             Disobedient in Denver

Dear Disobedient,
  Whenever I'm looking for good advice, I turn to the book of Proverbs. According to Proverbs 6:20-23, we should definitely listen to our parents and follow their advice. The things they teach us are like a light in the darkness. They help us find our way through life and avoid trouble. Sounds like good advice to me!

WHAT'S OUR NUMBER?

499.

I WISH I'D BROUGHT A SNACK.

Before Solomon became king,
God told him to ask for anything he wanted.
Solomon asked for wisdom, and God gave it to him.
That's why so many people came to King Solomon for advice.
He put some of his best advice in a Bible book called "Proverbs."

Next we visited Isaiah the prophet. A prophet was a person who received special messages from God about events in the future. God told Isaiah about the birth of Jesus more than 400 years before it happened!

THE MESSIAH WILL BE FROM KING DAVID'S FAMILY. HE WILL GROW UP IN NAZARETH...

HOW DOES HE *DO* THAT?

DO YOU THINK HE KNOWS WHO'LL WIN OUR NEXT SOCCER GAME?

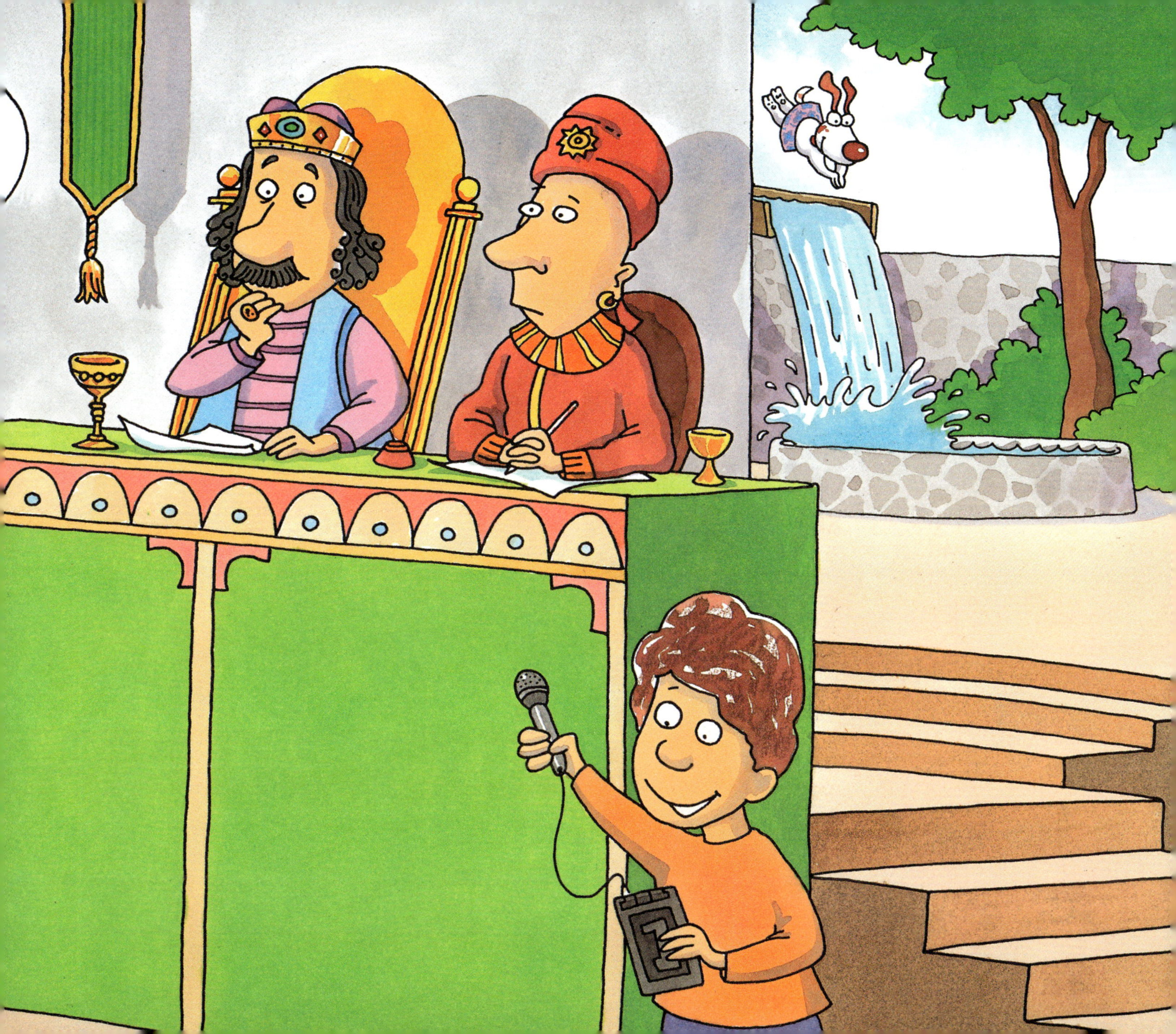

Isaiah wrote down all the messages that God gave to him.
He wanted everyone to hear what God had to say.
Today we can read in our Bibles what Isaiah
and the other prophets wrote about!

DO YOU THINK THEY'RE GOING TO BETHLEHEM TO VISIT JESUS?
BUT JESUS WON'T BE BORN FOR 400 YEARS!
THEN I HOPE THEY TAKE THEIR TIME.
BETHLEHEM OR BUST!

So far, we've had some great interviews with Moses, David, Solomon, and Isaiah. But all of their books are in the Old Testament. We knew that if we really wanted to write a great story, we needed to visit some New Testament writers, too.

Old Testament
The Bible books written before Jesus was born

New Testament
The Bible books written after Jesus was born

Next we stopped to see Matthew.
We told Gizmo to park the time machine very carefully.
Matthew was busy writing and we didn't want to disturb him.

WHAT'S HE DOING?

Matthew was writing the story of Jesus' life.
He wrote about the places Jesus went, the lessons Jesus taught,
and all the wonderful things Jesus did.

HE'S LISTENING TO SOMETHING.

I DON'T HEAR ANYTHING.

Matthew said writing his book was hard work, but God was guiding him all the way through it. That way, Matthew wouldn't make any mistakes! God helped every Bible writer know what to say.

AND WHEN JESUS WAS 12 YEARS OLD HIS FAMILY WENT TO JERUSALEM...

IF I DON'T STUDY, WILL GOD GUIDE ME ON MY NEXT TEST?

I WOULDN'T COUNT ON IT.

Time Travel Tribune

Bible Writers Helped by God When Writing Books

While visiting Matthew, our reporters made a very important discovery—every Bible writer has been guided by God!

"I'm very glad that God helped me write my book," said Matthew. "I'm just a human being, which means I can make mistakes or forget things easily. But God never makes any mistakes. With his guidance, I know that everything I'm writing is 100% true!"

Time Travelers Visit Bible Write

Our next interview was with Luke, who wrote the book of Acts. Acts is about the people God used to start the very first churches. It's full of shipwrecks and snakebites, earthquakes and angels, and soldiers and swords.

THE APOSTLE LUKE WROTE THE BOOK OF ACTS IN ABOUT 70 AD.

THIS IS AMAZING STUFF!

WHAT'S MOST AMAZING IS THAT IT'S ALL TRUE!

SCENES FROM ACTS BY LUKE

Luke told us exciting stories about the early Christians. They sure were brave people!
We could have stayed and listened to him all day, but we still had two more Bible writers to visit.

Book Review
by Shawn

Hello, book lovers! My review for this issue is about one of the most exciting books in the Bible—the book of Acts.

This book tells the story of people like Peter, Paul, Barnabas, and many others who risked their lives to start new churches all over the world.

The book of Acts is an action-packed adventure you shouldn't miss. I couldn't put it down for a second!

If you're one of those people who think the Bible is a boring book, check out Acts! It will change your mind.

At our next stop, we landed outside a Roman prison. After the guards let us inside, we got to meet Paul. He was one of the greatest Bible writers of all time!
PAUL, A SERVANT OF JESUS CHRIST, CALLED TO BE AN APOSTLE AND SET APART FOR THE GOSPEL
HOW DO YOU SPELL "SERVANT"?

Paul was in prison because he preached about Jesus. He spent his time writing important letters to churches and friends in other cities. Many of those letters became books in the Bible!

"DON'T WORRY, GIZMO. THIS ISN'T THE DOG POUND."

Books That Paul Wrote

Romans	Titus
Galatians	Philemon
Ephesians	1 Corinthians
Philippians	2 Corinthians
Colossians	1 Thessalonians
1 Timothy	2 Thessalonians
2 Timothy	

Our final stop was an island called Patmos. We wanted to interview John, the author of the book of Revelation.

"NEXT TO THE GOLDEN STREETS IS A RIVER..."

John had been arrested for talking about Jesus. But instead of being put in prison, like Paul, John was sent away to this lonely island. He wrote the book of Revelation after God gave him a peek into Heaven.

"HEAVEN SOUNDS LIKE A WONDERFUL PLACE!"

"AND GOD MADE IT JUST FOR US!"

"WHY CAN'T GIZMO JUST PLAY FETCH LIKE OTHER DOGS?"

It was finally time to head home.
When we got back to Shawn's house,
everyone hurried to write about our trip!
And Andy hurried to the kitchen to get a snack.

DEADLINE: 2:30 PM

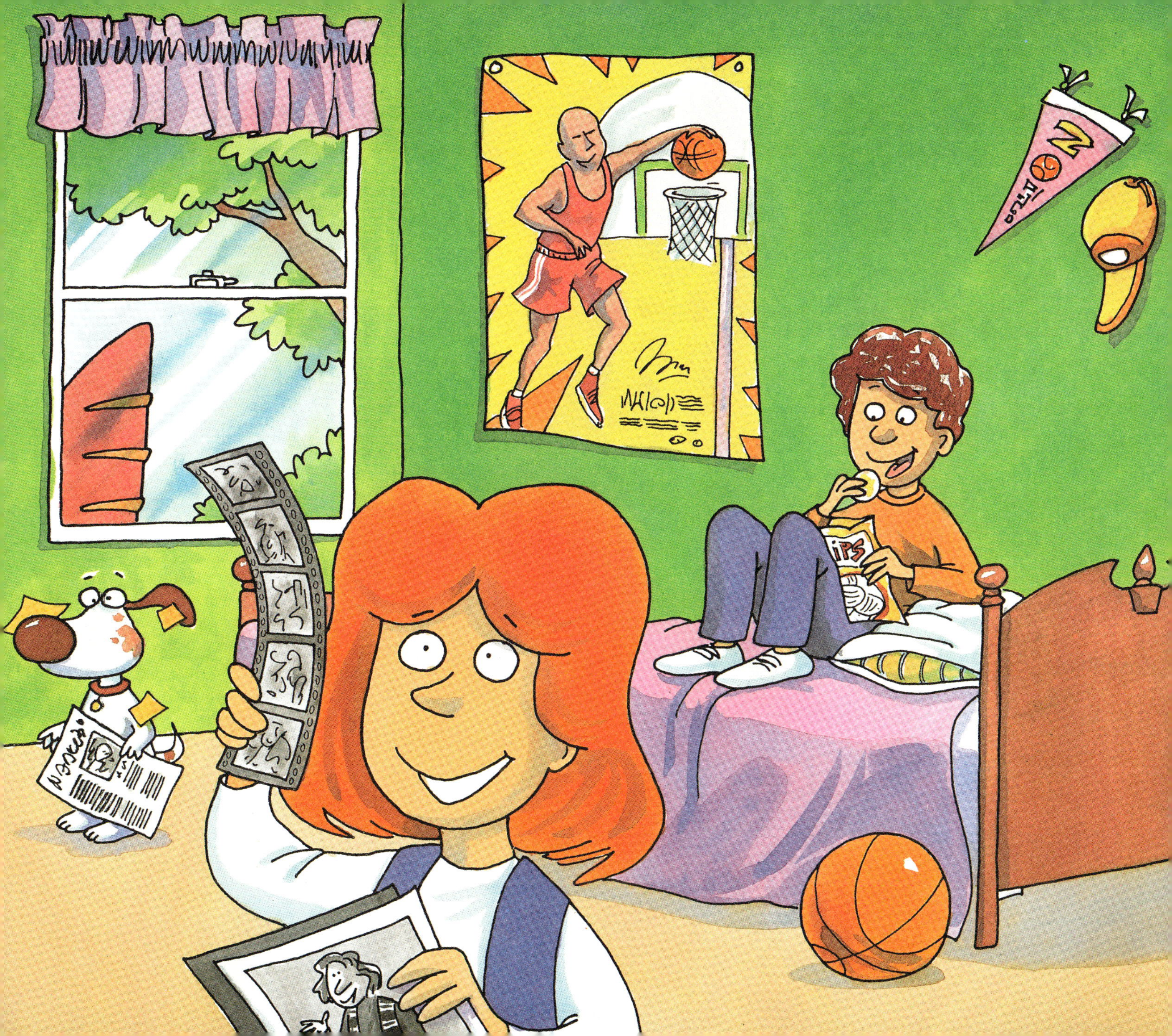

TIME TRAVEL TRIBUNE

Special Edition — All the History That's Fit to Visit — Just 25¢

Time Travelers Visit Bible Writers

Welcome to a special edition of the *Time Travel Tribune*. This issue is all about Bible writers. Our four ace reporters (and one ace dog) interviewed some of the many people who wrote the books of the Bible.

We started with the Old Testament, where we met Moses, David, Solomon, and Isaiah. Then it was on to the New Testament, where we had the chance to meet with Matthew, Luke, Paul, and John.

God helped over forty different people write the sixty-six books of the Bible. They included kings, shepherds, fishermen, doctors, prophets, and lots more!

But the best thing about the Bible is that it was written for YOU! God wanted you to learn all about him and how much he loves you. It's like God's personal letter to you. So don't just let your Bible sit on the shelf. Check it out!

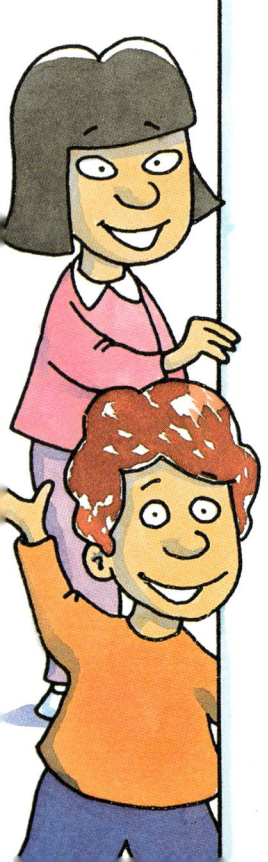